The
United
Nations

Preamble to the Charter of the United Nations

We the peoples of the United Nations determined
to save succeeding generations from the scourge of war, which twice in our lifetime
has brought untold sorrow to mankind,
and
to reaffirm faith in fundamental human rights, in the dignity and worth of the human person, in the equal rights of men and women and of nations large and small,
and
to establish conditions under which justice and respect for the obligations arising
from treaties and other sources of international law can be maintained,
and
to promote social progress and better standards of life in larger freedom,

And for these ends
to practice tolerance and live together in peace with one another as good neighbors,
and
to unite our strength to maintain international peace and security,
and
to ensure, by the acceptance of principles and the institution of methods, that armed
force shall not be used, save in the common interest,
and
to employ international machinery for the promotion of the economic
and social advancement of all peoples,

Have resolved to combine our efforts to accomplish these aims.

Accordingly, our respective Governments, through representatives assembled in the
city of San Francisco, who have exhibited their full powers found to be in good and
due form, have agreed to the present Charter of the United Nations and do hereby
establish an international organization to be known as the United Nations.

The United Nations

ANN ARMBRUSTER

A First Book
FRANKLIN WATTS
A Division of Grolier Publishing
New York / London / Hong Kong / Sydney
Danbury, Connecticut

Cover and Interior Design by Molly Heron
Cover photograph copyright ©: The United Nations
Photographs copyright ©: The Gamma Liaison Network: pp. 6, 24 (both J.
M. Turpin), 37 (Simon Walker/FSP), 38 (Christian Vioujard); Bettmann
Archive: p. 9; Reuters/Bettmann: pp. 17, 19, 52, 56; UPI/Bettmann: p. 27, top
left; U.S. Army Signal Corps.: p. 11; Harry S. Truman Library: p. 12; The
United Nations: pp. 16, 32 (both John Issac), 23, 27, 28, 30, 33 (Lois Conner),
35, 42, 45, 47, 49, 59; A/P Wide World Photos: p. 20

Library of Congress Cataloging-in-Publication Data

Armbruster, Ann.
The United Nations / Ann Armbruster.
p. cm. — (A First book)
Includes bibliographical references and index.
Summary: Discusses the United Nations, from its inception in 1945 to its
responsibility, fifty years later, as an international organization dedicated to
peace, justice, and economic equality.
ISBN 0-531-20201-1
1. United Nations—Juvenile literature. [1. United Nations.]
I. Title. II. Series
JX1977.Z8A76 1995
341.23—dc20   95-11292
CIP AC

Contents

NEA-BISSAU
GUATEM
GRENADA
BOTS
BOLIVIA
BHU
SANDA
TURKEY
TUNISIA
ANDA
VICE-CHAIRMAN

1

The Birth of the United Nations

Zaire, Israel, Kuwait, Russia, the United States, France, and Guatemala are countries with their own cultures, histories, governments, and languages. These diverse countries have one thing in common: they all belong to the United Nations.

On October 24, 1995, this community of nations—representing 185 countries on all seven continents—celebrated the fiftieth anniversary of its official existence. During the United Nations' first fifty years, countries all over the world worked together to search for solutions to worldwide problems.

At the United Nations, the largest intergovernmental organization in the world, representatives from 185 countries gather to have their voices heard.

When people think of the United Nations, they think of a global community that settles disputes peacefully and fairly, shares in the bounty of the Earth, and cooperates to solve problems. The founders of the United Nations hoped that an atmosphere of trust and communication would help achieve these goals. Some of their efforts succeeded and some failed.

TREATY OF VERSAILLES

After more than four years of fierce fighting that involved most of the world's great powers, an armistice, or truce, declared the end of World War I on November 11, 1918. Although the United States did not enter the war until 1917, over 116,00 American lives were lost.

In 1919, delegates from thirty-two countries assembled at the Palace of Versailles, near the city of Paris, to sign a formal peace treaty. These nations, torn apart by World War I, were looking for ways to preserve world peace. One part of this treaty, presented by the U.S. president Woodrow Wilson, provided for a group of

From left to right, Vittorio Orlando of Italy, David Lloyd George of Great Britain, Georges Clemenceau of France, and Woodrow Wilson sit for a picture in 1919 at the Paris Peace Conference.

countries to form a League of Nations. For membership in this association, nations were bound to come to the aid of any member nation threatened by an aggressor.

There was strong opposition to President Wilson's peace plan in the United States. Many members of Congress were isolationists—people who believed the country should stay out of world affairs—and, without the necessary votes in Congress, the treaty was never approved. Although Woodrow Wilson was awarded the Nobel Peace Prize in 1920 for his efforts, he was bitterly disappointed by the failure.

THE LEAGUE OF NATIONS

The League of Nations was formed without the United States in 1919 to promote international peace and security. In the 1920s and 1930s, the League succeeded in settling minor disputes but failed to stop the aggression of the major world powers. The first international organization devoted to worldwide peace was dissolved in 1946, but served as a model for its successor—the United Nations.

THE UN FOUNDING

The lessons of the next world war, which lasted from 1939 to 1945, were too severe to ignore. The costliest

The devastation and mass destruction of World War II
shocked the nations of the world into considering peaceful
alternatives to armed conflict.

On June 26, 1945, the UN Charter was signed. Secretary of State Edward R. Stettinius, Jr., signs for the United States while U.S. delegates and President Harry S. Truman (*left*) look on.

war in history, World War II left over 50 million dead, and 250,000 American lives were lost. When the atomic bomb was dropped on Hiroshima and Nagasaki in 1945, instantly killing about 250,000 civilians, even isolationists realized the need for a league of nations dedicated to peace.

The initial moves for a new organization were formed even before the United States entered World War II. On August 14, 1941, President Franklin D. Roosevelt and Prime Minister Winston Churchill of Great Britain met to sign the Atlantic Charter, which proclaimed common moral principles for a peaceful world.

In 1942, representatives from twenty-six countries signed a Declaration of United Nations, pledging themselves to support the Atlantic Charter. Further conferences among the Big Powers at Dumbarton Oaks in Washington, D.C., and Yalta in the Crimea led to the formation of the United Nations.

On June 26, 1945, representatives from fifty countries met in the San Francisco Opera House to draft a Charter of the United Nations. The United Nations (UN) was officially born on October 24, 1945, the day the Charter went into effect. Every year on this day United Nations Day is celebrated.

2

A Family of Nations

When the United Nations was formed in 1945, this family of nations wanted better lives for all the citizens of the world. To achieve this purpose, it designed the Charter of the United Nations with six main divisions, or organs. They are the General Assembly, the Security Council, the Economic and Social Council (ECOSOC), the Trusteeship Council, the International Court of Justice, and the Secretariat. Each of these organs has a specific purpose.

GENERAL ASSEMBLY

The General Assembly has some control over all the other UN organs. It is the only UN body with representatives from all 185 member states. Regardless of size, population, wealth, or power, each nation has only one vote in Assembly voting.

The General Assembly is sometimes considered a world parliament, but it has no power to enforce its decisions on individual countries. Although Assembly decisions have no binding legal power, they carry the weight of world opinion.

The General Assembly meets every year from mid-September to mid-December. If a state of emergency exists, a meeting can be called at any time. For decisions on important issues, such as budgetary affairs and matters of security, a majority two-thirds' vote is required. No nation has the power to veto an act of the Assembly.

Dubbed the "town meeting of the world," the Assembly also sets standards for the world by passing conventions, treaties, proclamations, and declarations. Some passed during the first fifty years of United Nations include the

- Treaty on the Non-Proliferation of Nuclear Weapons
- Declaration on the Prevention of Nuclear Catastrophe
- Declaration on the Right of People to Peace
- Universal Declaration of Human Rights
- Convention on the Elimination of All Forms of Racial Discrimination
- Charter of Economic Rights and Duties of States
- Convention on the Rights of the Child
- United Nations Principles for Older Persons
- World Charter for Nature

The General Assembly meets in this brightly lit rotunda at UN headquarters in New York City. On either side of the UN seal are electronic vote tabulation boards and two rows of television, photo, and interpreters' booths.

Madeleine K. Albright, appointed in 1993, is the current U.S. representative to the United Nations. She is the country's twenty-first UN ambassador.

SECURITY COUNCIL

The main responsibility of the Security Council is to maintain international peace and security. The Council has fifteen members, five of whom have permanent seats: China, France, Great Britain, Russia, and the United States. These five countries also have the power to veto any decision made by the Council. The ten remaining members are elected for two-year terms by the General Assembly.

The Security Council can ask for economic sanctions against a nation, investigate disputes between countries, or seek military action against an aggressor. Once a decision is made, all member nations are obligated under the Charter to abide by it. Since emergency meetings of the Council can be called at any time, a representative from each member country must always be available.

In order to pass a resolution, nine Council members must vote "yes." If any of the five permanent Council members vote "no," it is called a veto, and the resolution does not pass.

ECONOMIC AND SOCIAL COUNCIL (ECOSOC)

The Economic and Social Council is the social worker of the UN family. Its specialized agencies direct a variety of activities. They are responsible for promoting the im-

Members of the UN Security Council meet around this horseshoe-shaped table in a special chamber of the Conference Building. Interpreters and other UN staff work at the long table in the center.

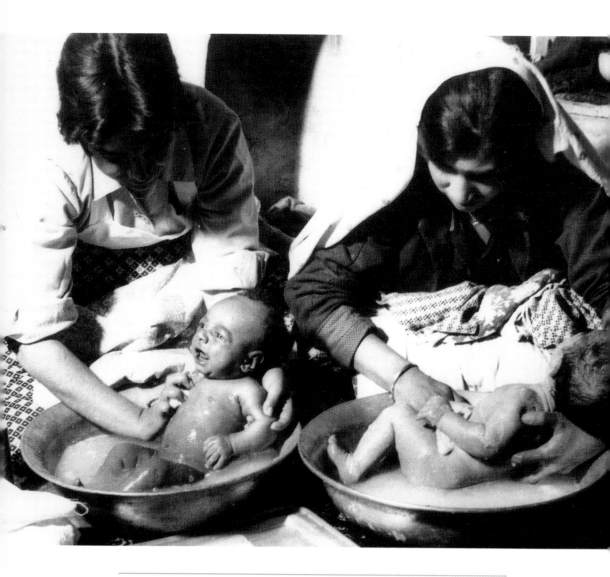

The United Nations coordinates work of many kinds in many countries. In this photo, a UN health worker demonstrates the baby bath to a mother of twins in Iran.

provement of the way people live. They coordinate the economic and social work of the United Nations and encourage educational and cultural cooperation among member countries.

The fifty-four members of ECOSOC are elected by the General Assembly for three-year terms. Eighteen are elected each year. ECOSOC meets at least twice a year.

It handles a wide range of economic and social needs in response to the world's changing political structure. In 1945, much of the world's population still lived in territories governed by other countries. As these territories became developing nations, their social problems increased. They needed help to educate their people, improve their health services, and modernize their economic and social resources. ECOSOC has helped many developing nations stand on their own feet.

Trusteeship Council

After World War I, colonies belonging to Germany were placed under the authority of the League of Nations. When the United Nations took over the League's responsibility of protecting these colonies, they were given to various countries that promised to rule them fairly. The Trusteeship Council was also established to oversee territories that were not self-governing at the end of World War II. These colonies were called trust territories.

The main purpose of the Trusteeship Council is to help guide the people living in the trust territories toward self-government and independence. It meets at least once a year.

Its work has been mostly a success. Only one of the original eleven trusteeships remains—the Trust Territory of the Pacific Islands, which is administered by the United States. The others either attained independence or joined neighboring independent countries.

INTERNATIONAL COURT OF JUSTICE

The International Court of Justice, often called the World Court, is the main judicial organ of the United Nations. Located in The Hague in the Netherlands, it is the only major UN division not in the United States.

The World Court is made up of fifteen judges. They are elected by the General Assembly and the Security Council, each voting independently. Judges are chosen on the basis of qualifications, not nationality, for a term of nine years and may be re-elected. They cannot engage in any other occupation while serving on the Court.

The principal legal systems of the world are represented here. The Court hears arguments from countries, not individuals, and has no power to enforce its decisions. It hands down its rulings by majority vote. Upon occasion, the Court has given advisory opinions to the General Assembly and the Security Council.

This impressive building, called the Peace Palace,
houses the World Court.

Some of the most important members of the UN staff are the interpreters who enable representatives from different countries to communicate. The six official UN languages are Arabic, Chinese, English, French, Russian, and Spanish.

The Secretariat is the administrative organ of the United Nations. Run by the secretary-general, this division carries out the programs and policies laid out by the other UN organs.

The Secretariat staff is made up of 16,000 people from 150 countries. These people manage the day-to-day activities of the United Nations in New York and around the world. The international civil servants take an oath not to accept instruction from any government outside the United Nations in accomplishing their duties. Among the staff are personnel officers, administrators, economists, linguists, legal experts, and librarians, along with maintenance engineers, clerks, and secretaries.

As the United Nations has grown, so have the duties of the Secretariat, the backbone of the United Nations. As the late former secretary-general Dag Hammarskjöld put it, the Secretariat "can put before member governments findings which will influence their activities."

The secretary-general is the United Nation's chief executive officer and is appointed by the General Assembly every five years with the option of being re-elected. This spokesperson to the world has the right to bring before the Security Council any matter that he considers a threat to international peace and security. The secretary-general acts as a negotiator when there are conflicts among countries, will order UN troops to the world's trouble spots, and uses the skills of diplomacy in this most demanding job.

UN secretary-generals have been outstanding people of achievement in their own right. The Norwegian Trygve Lie (1946–52) was the first secretary-general. Next came the Swede Dag Hammarskjöld (1953–61), the Burmese U Thant (1962–71), the Austrian Kurt Waldheim (1972–82), and the Peruvian Javier Pérez de Cuéllar (1982–91). Today's secretary-general is the Egyptian Boutros Boutros-Ghali, who has held office since 1992.

The first six UN secretary-generals: (from left to right) Trygve Lie, Dag Hammarskjöld, U Thant, Kurt Waldheim, Javier Pérez de Cuéllar, Boutros Boutros-Ghali

A UN tour guide shows a group of young visitors
The Golden Rule, a mosaic by the well-known
American artist Norman Rockwell.

3

A Home for the United Nations

Where can you visit international territory without leaving the United States; take a tour given in twenty-five different languages of the only buildings owned by the citizens of the world; see the hall where the largest gatherings of world leaders take place; eat in an international restaurant; and buy collector's stamps to mail letters home from a world post office? Only at UN headquarters.

UN HEADQUARTERS

In 1945, after the UN Charter was signed in San Francisco, the General Assembly voted to place the permanent UN headquarters in the United States. Many different sites were considered, but a public-spirited oil magnate, John D. Rockefeller, Jr., helped make the fi-

nal decision. His offer of $8.5 million to buy an 18-acre (7-ha) site on the shore of the East River in New York City was accepted immediately. New York City gave the United Nations the extra land needed to complete the project. Officially, the site itself is international, not American, territory.

The headquarters of the United Nations is located on what used to be known as the Turtle Bay area. It was here that the British hanged Nathan Hale for spying on them during the Revolutionary War. The complex has four buildings: the low-domed General Assembly Building, the 39-story, glass-and-aluminum Secretariat Building, the Dag Hammarskjöld Library, and the rectangular Conference Building along the river.

Construction costs, not including the library, amounted to $67 million, almost all of which was financed interest-free by the United States. The Dag Hammarskjöld Library, at a cost of $6.6 million, was a gift from the Ford Foundation, a charity set up by Henry Ford, the auto manufacturer.

This view of the UN headquarters includes the Secretariat Building, the tall structure in the center; the Conference Building, front; the General Assembly Building, right; and the Dag Hammarskjöld Library, left.

Since the founding of the United Nations, its blue-and-white flag
has become a familiar sight around the world.

TOURING THE UNITED NATIONS

Over the years, more than thirty million visitors have
taken guided tours of UN headquarters. They come to
see some of the daily activities of the United Nations in
action, tour the grounds of this famous building, and
marvel at its fascinating treasures inside.

Pictured here is a section of a stained-glass memorial to Dag
Hammarskjöld and the fifteen others who lost their lives in a
plane crash in Africa. It is a gift from the UN staff and Marc
Chagall, the French artist who executed the work.

As you enter the gates of the UN Plaza, you see flags of UN member nations displayed in alphabetical order. The blue-and-white UN flag flies higher than the others. It features two olive branches, as symbols of peace, and a view of the Earth as seen from the North Pole.

In the lobby of the visitors' entrance you will see a gift from the Soviet Union — a life-size model of *Sputnik*, the first space satellite. Then a 200-pound (91-kg) gold pendulum suspended from the ceiling will catch your attention. The pendulum appears to move but, in fact, it is the Earth that is moving. This unique object was a gift from the Netherlands.

Since 1945, the United Nations has acquired an outstanding art collection. All the art objects, which are gifts from various countries and friends of the UN, are dedicated to peace. Sculpture, murals, rugs, and paintings are just some of the United Nations' treasures.

The Meditation Room, located in the General Assembly Building, contains a great slab of raw iron ore that represents timelessness and strength. From the Swedish government, the 6-ton (5,443-kg) object dominates the quiet space.

In the gardens, northwest of the Secretariat Building, is the Japanese Peace Bell, which was crafted from coins of six countries. The bell stands on a base of Judean marble, a gift of Israel.

The grounds and buildings of the United Nations are filled with gifts from member countries, such as this Japanese Peace Bell.

As you continue the tour of the UN buildings, you will find many art treasures reflecting the hopes of all the UN countries for world peace.

4

A Better Life for All People

One of the goals laid out in the UN Charter is "to promote social progress and better standards of life." In other words, the Charter calls on the United Nations to work for improved living standards for the people of all countries. The sharp division between rich and poor nations within the United Nations is often seen as a long-term threat to world peace.

To promote social justice for all, the United Nations created numerous agencies staffed by thousands of employees from all over the world. These workers include doctors, nurses, scientists, teachers, technicians, lawyers, economists, and agricultural specialists, among many others. The work they do in less-developed countries is one step toward bringing peace, health, and prosperity to all.

A goodwill ambassador for UNICEF, American actress
Audrey Hepburn tended to sick and starving children
in developing countries all over the world, including
Somalia (shown here), before her death in 1993.

In 1995, the World Health Organization cosponsored a worldwide AIDS conference in Paris. Officials from various countries pose with UN secretary-general Boutros-Ghali.

United Nations Children's Fund (UNICEF)

In 1946, UNICEF, originally named the United Nations International Children's Emergency Fund, was started as an emergency project to help children in postwar Europe and China. The results were so impressive that it was made a permanent UN agency in 1953. UNICEF was awarded the Nobel Peace Prize in 1965. It is supported by contributions from governments and private donations.

In the United States, UNICEF is often associated with Halloween and trick-or-treating. Every year, thousands of children go door-to-door collecting donations to the Children's Fund instead of candy. It also raises money from the sale of UNICEF greeting cards. This agency carries on many different hunger, health, and educational campaigns and programs to help needy children throughout the world. UNICEF's child inoculations, for example, have dramatically lowered the death rate of children.

World Health Organization (WHO)

This organization has a primary goal to work toward health care for all people by the year 2000. For countries to prosper, their citizens must be healthy and productive. Increasing and improving worldwide access to health services is an ambitious task, but the success of WHO's work so far has been encouraging.

WHO was established after World War II, with its headquarters in Geneva, Switzerland. It sponsors and monitors international health research and programs. Among its projects have been the elimination of smallpox as a threatening disease and the formation of primary health-service organizations in developing countries.

In cooperation with UNICEF, WHO targeted six diseases—measles, diphtheria, tetanus, whooping cough, poliomyelitis, and tuberculosis—that kill an estimated five million children in the developing world each year. Their Expanded Program on Immunization has helped and should continue to help achieve the goal of universal child immunization against these six diseases.

UN Educational, Scientific, and Cultural Organization (UNESCO)

Headquartered in Paris, UNESCO was formed on the principle that if people have a better understanding of one another, they will be less likely to go to war. UNESCO encourages countries to share their varied knowledge and unique culture with other peoples of the world. It operates in close partnership with national groups, offering technical assistance and help.

One of this group's major goals is to wipe out illiteracy. If illiteracy continues to rise, by the year 2000 there will be one billion people in the world who are unable to read. UNESCO helps interested governments to organize school systems and teacher-training institutes. UNESCO's teachers, scientists, and technicians work mainly in the fields of education, natural science, culture, and communication.

HUMAN RIGHTS

All UN members are bound by the UN Charter "to reaffirm faith in fundamental rights, in the dignity and worth of the human person, in the equal rights of men and women, and of nations, large and small." In this proclamation, the Charter refers to human rights but does not define them.

To provide a definition for the term *human rights* and set a standard for all nations to respect, the United Nations adopted a Universal Declaration of Human Rights on December 10, 1948. This day is celebrated as Human Rights Day in many countries. To honor the Declaration, the United Nations issued special postage stamps.

Since some UN countries have different ideas as to what human rights are, the Declaration had to include basic economic and social rights as well as civil and political rights. People from the Western nations tend to take for granted certain rights—rights that people from less-fortunate countries do not have.

Eleanor Roosevelt, wife of the U.S. president Franklin D. Roosevelt, worked hard to promote human rights all over the world. She was once asked where such rights

41

begin. She responded: "In small places—close to home—so close and so small that they cannot be seen on any map of the world. Yet they are the world of the individual person: the neighborhood he lives in, the school or college he attends, the factory, farm, or office where he works. Such are the places where [each] man, woman, and child seeks justice, equal opportunity, equal dignity, without discrimination. Unless these rights have a meaning there, they have little meaning anywhere."

WORLD BANK

Officially the International Bank for Reconstruction and Development (IBRD), the World Bank supervises the lending of money to UN countries for development projects. This organization, along with the International Monetary Fund (IMF), was set up after World War II to provide countries affected by the war with funds to rebuild. Since then, other countries in need have turned to the World Bank to finance public utilities, agriculture, and community development.

Eleanor Roosevelt holds the Universal Declaration of Human Rights. As chair of the UN Commission on Human Rights, Mrs. Roosevelt was instrumental in the creation and adoption of the Declaration.

Other UN Agencies

Food and Agriculture Organization (FAO)
Works to improve production and distribution of food.

International Atomic Energy Agency (IAEA)
Encourages safe and peaceful uses of nuclear energy worldwide.

International Civil Aviation Organization (ICAO)
Promotes safe and orderly growth of general air transportation.

International Labor Organization (ILO)
Works to improve working and living conditions worldwide.

International Maritime Organization (IMO)
Promotes cooperation in shipping practices and regulations.

International Telecommunications Union (ITU)
Encourages nations to share radio, telephone, telegraph, and satellite communications technology.

United Nations Environment Program (UNEP)
Monitors environmental conditions and regulations.

Universal Postal Union (UPU)
Organizes international cooperation in mail delivery.

World Meteorological Organization (WMO)
Promotes cooperation among countries in forecasting and analyzing weather conditions.

THE UNITED NATIONS SYSTEM

SECRETARIAT

INTERNATIONAL COURT OF JUSTICE

TRUSTEESHIP COUNCIL

GENERAL ASSEMBLY

SECURITY COUNCIL

ECONOMIC AND SOCIAL COUNCIL

Main and other sessional committees

Standing committees and ad hoc bodies

Other subsidiary organs and related bodies

UNRWA
United Nations Relief and Works Agency for Palestine Refugees in the Near East

UNDOF
United Nations Disengagement Observer Force

UNFICYP
United Nations Peace-keeping Force in Cyprus

UNIFIL
United Nations Interim Force in Lebanon

UNMOGIP
United Nations Military Observer Group in India and Pakistan

UNTSO
United Nations Truce Supervision Organization

Military Staff Committees

Standing committee and ad hoc bodies

INSTRAW
International Research and Training Institute for the Advancement of Women

UNCTAD
United Nations Conference on Trade and Development

UNDP
United Nations Development Programme

UNEP
United Nations Environment Programme

UNFPA
United Nations Fund for Population Activities

UNHCR
Office of the United Nations High Commissioner for Refugees

UNICEF
United Nations Children's Fund

UNITAR
United Nations Institute for Training and Research

UNU
United Nations University

WFC
World Food Council

WFP
Joint UN/FAO World Food Programme

*UNDRO
Office of the United Nations Disaster Relief Co-ordinator

* A unit of the Secretariat

REGIONAL COMMISSIONS

Economic Commission for Africa (ECA)

Economic Commission for Europe (ECE)

Economic Commission for Latin America and the Caribbean (ECLAC)

Economic and Social Commission for Asia and the Pacific (ESCAP)

Economic and Social Commission for Western Asia (ESCWA)

FUNCTIONAL COMMISSIONS

Commission for Social Development

Commission on Human Rights

Commission on Narcotic Drugs

Commission on the Status of Women

Population Commission

Statistical Commission

SESSIONAL AND STANDING COMMITTEES

EXPERT, AD HOC AND RELATED BODIES

IAEA
International Atomic Energy Agency

ILO
International Labour Organisation

FAO
Food and Agriculture Organization of the United Nations

UNESCO
United Nations Educational, Scientific and Cultural Organization

WHO
World Health Organization

IDA
International Development Association

IBRD
International Bank for Reconstruction and Development (World Bank)

IFC
International Finance Corporation

IMF
International Monetary Fund

ICAO
International Civil Aviation Organization

UPU
Universal Postal Union

ITU
International Telecommunication Union

WMO
World Meteorological Organization

IMO
International Maritime Organization

WIPO
World Intellectual Property Organization

IFAD
International Fund for Agricultural Development

UNIDO
United Nations Industrial Development Organization

GATT
General Agreement on Tariffs and Trade

Principal organs of the United Nations

Other United Nations programmes and organs (representative list only)

Specialized agencies and other autonomous organizations within the system

This chart outlines the organization of the United Nations.

5

The Peacekeepers

In 1988, UN peacekeeping forces won the Nobel Peace Prize. It was a remarkable year for UN peace efforts. UN soldiers played a vital part in the Soviet withdrawal from Afghanistan, the cease-fire in the Iran–Iraq War, and the departure of Cuban troops from Angola. There was talk of "an outbreak of peace" in the world and UN efforts were applauded.

However, some questions still remain about the present and future of UN peacekeeping troops. What is peacekeeping exactly? Who pays for these forces? What do peacekeepers need to know? Is the United Nations overextending itself?

Over the years, UN soldiers have played many roles. In this 1960 photo, a member of the UN force from Ethiopia on duty in Congo (now Zaire) takes time out to play with a friend.

What Is Peacekeeping?

In 1948, the UN Security Council sent unarmed military observers to the Middle East after the Arab–Israeli War of 1948–49. These observers supervised the truce between the Israelis and Arabs. They were also the first UN peacekeepers.

For many years, the United Nations has used its peacekeeping troops to stabilize international discord while diplomatic efforts are made to resolve the conflict. Although the UN Charter does not mention "peacekeeping," it refers to rejecting the use of force, the peaceful settlement of disputes, and a unified response to aggression. UN peacekeeping operations help keep countries from resorting to force to resolve their disagreements.

Peacekeeping operations are established with the consent of the Security Council. Their purpose is to prevent fighting, police cease-fires, act as a buffer between hostile forces, or serve as observers. With a light-blue helmet for easy identification, UN soldiers follow a different set of rules from typical soldiers. UN peacekeeping soldiers are under the authority of the UN secretary-

Although their first obligation is to peace, UN peacekeepers must train for self-defense.

general and the Security Council; they achieve results through negotiations and persuasion, not force; and they use weapons only in self-defense.

WHO PAYS FOR PEACEKEEPING FORCES?

All UN members share the costs of maintaining the current 72,000 peacekeepers in their seventeen operations throughout the world. The five permanent members of the Security Council pay larger shares than the other countries. The peacekeeping bill accounts for more than one-third of the total UN debt. As of 1994, the United States was paying 30.4 percent of UN peacekeeping costs.

The unparalleled expansion of UN peacekeeping operations has led to a financial crisis within the organization. Countries routinely withhold payment for peacekeeping because of a political situation or domestic financial strain. In 1993, unpaid UN peacekeeping bills totaled nearly $1.5 billion. That same year, the United Nations spent some $3.8 billion on peacekeeping, five times the amount spent only two years earlier.

WHAT DO PEACEKEEPERS NEED TO KNOW?

American soldiers learn the art of peacekeeping in northern Bavarian Germany where the U.S. Army has converted 44,000 acres (17,806 ha) into an outdoor classroom. The soldiers are confronted with situations ranging from hungry refugees begging for food to angry civilians accusing peacekeepers of favoritism. Role-playing teaches soldiers how to react in crucial situations. If their role is that of a peacekeeper confronted by an irate local citizen, they must quickly decide whether to argue with the person or diffuse the situation with careful questions. As one soldier explained, "Peacekeeping is rough. You have to be a politician."

IS THE UNITED NATIONS OVEREXTENDING ITSELF?

The end of the Cold War signaled a change in the role of the United Nations in resolving international disputes. Countries no longer fell into two spheres of influence: one led by the Soviet Union and one led by the United States. The warming of relations between the two superpowers would help the UN Security Council come to agreements on issues concerning the many regional conflicts that could require peacekeeping intervention.

All around the world, simmering disputes previously overshadowed by Cold War tensions have come to a boil. Many of these conflicts stem from human-rights abuses and religious differences. In the former Yugoslavia, national interests strive for superiority. In

Somalia, a global humanitarian response to famine becomes a military match. And in Rwanda, unequaled slaughter has killed refugees at the rate of one per minute.

The need for international peacekeeping efforts has rarely seemed so great. While UN involvement in conducting elections and setting up democratic structures in Cambodia, El Salvador, Eastern Europe, and Namibia have been largely successful, there are many more challenges ahead. The United Nations is being asked to take on a larger, sometimes impossible, role in building a peaceful and just world.

Here, a UN soldier gets out of an armored personnel carrier in the warring former Yugoslavia. With limited ability to maintain peace, UN peacekeepers have a difficult, often hopeless, job.

6

The United Nations Today and Tomorrow

The world has changed dramatically since the founding of the United Nations in 1945. The world order has changed, the map has changed, the economy has changed; and many new problems face the United Nations.

NEW WORLD ORDER

The end of colonialism and Soviet communism presented new opportunities for UN action and also new uncertainties. Rapidly changing world circumstances required a rethinking of UN policies and adaptations to these global changes.

In his Perspectives for the 1990s, the UN's fifth secretary-general, Javier Pérez de Cuéllar, noted, "It must be the common purpose to forge from . . . varied, sometimes contradictory, economic, social and political conditions, a global environment of sustained development, social justice and peace."

People everywhere question whether the traditional structures of governments are adequate for today's complex world. The competency of these governments is often eroded. With massive amounts of information available to all parts of the world, many citizens are looking beyond these governments for answers to their problems.

The United Nations worked well in the post-Cold War days. It ended conflicts in Cambodia, Nicaragua, El Salvador, Angola, and Afghanistan. The high point of these successes was the ejection of the Iraqi troops from Kuwait during the Persian Gulf War.

The world wanted and expected a lot from the United Nations. In the words of Secretary-General Boutros Boutros-Ghali, "Never before in its history has the United Nations been so action-oriented, so actively engaged, and so widely expected to respond to needs both immediate and pervasive."

Now the thin blue line of the UN staff is stretched to the breaking point. Resources are meager and demands are high. Efforts to make peace in Bosnia were blocked, there were ninety-one UN fatalities in Somalia, eleven UN soldiers were killed in Rwanda, and UN observers were forced to leave Haiti.

Blue-helmeted UN soldiers unload a shipment
of humanitarian aid.

UN Financial Crisis

At a time when world leaders are calling for a strengthening of UN power, a growing financial crisis is erupting within the organization. Much of the crisis arose from the growing demand for peacekeeping forces and the failure of member states to pay their assessments. In 1993, only seven of all the member nations paid their full share.

To reform the monetary mess, former secretary-general de Cuéllar suggested that (1) the United Nations charge interest as commercial rates on all overdue assessments, (2) the United Nations have the power to borrow money commercially, and (3) the United Nations establish a peacekeeping fund. Several critics of the United Nations added a fourth solution—the United Nations should decrease its bureaucracy and increase its efficiency to save money.

UN Achievements

These days, some people proclaim that the United Nations is a collection of outdated idealists. Others praise UN achievements, such as:

- Keeping international peace.
- Improving the quality of life through the World Health Organization.

- Saving children's lives through the UN Children's Fund.

- Helping to eliminate poverty through the UN Development Fund.

- Protecting the environment by extending international law into outer space and the sea.

- Placing the Universal Declaration of Human Rights high on the international agenda.

TODAY AND TOMORROW

Today developing nations are striving for a standard of living that developed nations take for granted. Great migrations of people are creating almost insurmountable problems, and countries are scrambling for a share of the Earth's resources. In the midst of this turmoil, the United Nations—with both its triumphs and defeats—remains the only international organization dedicated to peace, justice, and economic equality.

The future of the United Nations depends on the willingness and dedication of its member nations to work together and adapt to ever-changing situations. Its future as an effective global institution also depends greatly on the support of the citizens of all 185 UN countries. The United Nations can be a great parliament for peace or it can become just another failure in history.

During UN Plaza improvements made in the early 1950s,
this quotation from the Bible was inscribed as a reminder
of the United Nations' founding principles.

❧ For Further Information ❧

If you are planning a visit to UN Headquarters, located at First Avenue and 46th Street in New York City, you can take guided tours seven days a week (except Christmas and New Year's Day) from 9:15 A.M. to 4:45 P.M. For current information on prices, call (212) 963–7713. To make reservations for guided tours of fifteen people or more, call (212) 963–4440.

For more information about the UN Bookshop, which sells postcards, stationery, UN calendars, slides, and books, call (212) 963–7680.

To receive a complete catalog of UN publications, write or call United Nations Publications, Room DC2-853, 2 UN Plaza, New York, NY 10017; (212) 963–8302.

For specific requests for UN information materials, write or call Public Inquiries Unit, UN Department of Public Information, Room GA-057, UN Headquarters, New York, NY 10017; (212) 963–4475.

For a complete list of publications from UNA-USA, write or call UNA-USA, 485 Fifth Avenue, New York, NY 10017; (212) 697–3232.

For Further Reading

Jacobs, William J. *Search for Peace: The Story of the United Nations*. New York: Scribner Books for Young Readers, 1994.

Pollard, Michael. *United Nations*. New York: New Discovery Books, 1994.

Sheldon, Richard. *Dag Hammarskjöld*. New York: Chelsea House, 1987.

Stein, R. Conrad. *The Story of the United Nations*. Chicago: Childrens Press, 1986.

Woog, Adam. *United Nations*. San Diego: Lucent Books, 1994.

 Index

About the Author

Ann Armbruster has been an English teacher and a school librarian. She is the author of several Franklin Watts First Books, including *The American Flag*. Ms. Armbruster lives in Ohio, where she pursues her interest in history.